CW00431975

THE HIGHEST COMMON FACTOR

UNDERSTANDING THE GRACE PHENOMENON

The Highest Common Factor
© 2011 by Olayinka Dada

Published by Dunamis Press
P.O. Box 337, Chester, NY 10918

Library of Congress Control Number: 2010930676
ISBN-13:978-0-9822855-2-7
ISBN-10:0-9822855-2-3

Unless otherwise indicated, Scripture quotations are taken from the New King James Version. Copyright 1982, by Thomas Nelson, Inc. Used by permission. All rights reserved.

Scripture quotations marked MSG are taken from The Message. Copyright 1993, 1994, 1995, 1996, 2000, 2001, 2002. Used by permission of NavPress Publishing Group.

Scripture quotations marked NCV are taken from the New Century Version. © 2005 by Thomas Nelson, Inc. Used by permission. All rights reserved.

Scripture quotations marked NIV are taken from the Holy Bible, New International Version®. © 1973, 1978, 1984 Biblica. Used by permission of Zondervan. All rights reserved.

Scripture quotations marked NLT are taken from the Holy Bible, New Living Translation, Copyright 1996, 2004. Used by permission of Tyndale House Publishers, Inc., Wheaton, Illinois 60189. All rights reserved.

All rights reserved. No part of this book may be reproduced in any form without written permission from the author.

All the stories in this book are used by permission. To protect the privacy of those who shared their stories with the author, some names and details have been changed.

Book design by Leigh Anne Ference-Kaemmer

Printed in the United States of America

"The effect of grace upon an individual, place or thing cannot be denied; it speaks with the loudest of voices. It is boldly revealed in the life of that person. Without grace life is meaningless and worthless. The Highest Common Factor is a classic on the subject of grace. It is a must read for everyone who wishes to live with God's favor."

- APOSTLE FRIDAY A. IDAWOR
Secretary, Pentecostal Fellowship of Nigeria, Lagos

"Pastor Dada has again taken this generation on a tour of the almighty subject, called grace. Written in a forceful and insightful manner, the author explains that grace is a spiritual living force that gives a man sweatless triumph in the conflicts of life. In grace we live and move and have our total being. This is a must read classic for everyone who wants to ride on the tide of grace in this generation."

- OLABODE ADEOSUN
Author, Grace for the Race

"In this book, Dr. Dada brings out the grace factor in every sphere of the believer's life. Read this book if you want to conclude your race on earth with excellence and victory."

- PASTOR TOSIN MACAULEY
Regional Coordinator, RCCG Southern Africa 2 Region, Johannesburg

"When you read through this book, you will discover that grace has absolutely nothing to do with the individual who receives it, but an unmerited favor paid for by the death and resurrection of Christ. This book will greatly bless you."

- WILLIAM FEMI AWODELE,
Author, International Speaker, Omaha, Nebraska

"This book is a wealth of treasure for anyone who truly desires divine grace for supernatural open doors."

- BISHOP (DR.) YOMI ISIJOLA,
Logos Ministries, Port Harcourt, Nigeria

THE HIGHEST COMMON FACTOR

UNDERSTANDING THE GRACE PHENOMENON

OLAYINKA DADA, M.D.

Foreword by Dr. Samuel R. Chand

To my loving wife, Oluwatoyin Abimbola Dada.
We always have reasons to celebrate, testify and
appreciate the grace of God that brought us together.

CONTENTS

And of His fullness we have all received,
and grace for grace.

🌿 **John 1:16**

∽ Foreword ∼

GRACE—who can fully comprehend and describe it? GRACE—it is a noun, verb, adjective and other part of our language!

GRACE as a noun describes what it is. By definition grace can be a person, place or thing. As a person it is personified through Jesus and demonstrated through us. As a place it allows us to understand the true meaning of sanctuary or a safe place. As a thing we become stewards of grace. Grace is what you have.

GRACE as a verb asks us to act on it. We receive grace to do something with it. As soon as grace is deposited in our lives, we too must reach out and find people and places to deposit grace into. Grace is what you do.

GRACE as an adjective describes someone as graceful. It is the language of understanding all the nuances of grace. It is how you personify grace. Grace is who you are.

In his book, *THE HIGHEST COMMON FACTOR: Understanding the Grace Phenomenon* Dr. Olayinka Dada takes these and other facets of grace and helps us understand the multi-dimensional word we use so frequently—Grace.

May we all continue growing in GRACE!

GRACE to you.

Dr. Samuel R. Chand
www.samchand.com

∽ Foreword ∽

The Highest Common Factor is an exposition on the essence of grace as bestowed upon us by the Lord. Grace is often aptly described to us as an acronym, "Gods Riches At Christ's Expense." This is apt because we all could not afford it and yet God purchased it and gave it to us free of charge. However, this is as far as most people go in their journey of faith.

Pastor Dada eloquently tells us that grace wears many faces. For example, there is the grace bestowed upon a wounded and weary soldier to continue in his assignment; grace is needed to live a life acceptable to God; grace is needed to accommodate the unlovable; grace is needed for those heading into or already in the storms of life; grace is needed to excel spiritually, physically and financially; and grace is needed not only to start well but to finish well. Again, there is transferable grace; grace to receive and also give, and finally, the Christian must be a man or woman of grace.

Grace is mentioned in the scriptures in varying dimensions and you have great grace (Acts 4:38), abundant grace (Romans 5:17), exceeding grace (2 Corinthians 9:14) and manifold grace (1 Peter 4: 10). May we never forget the lyrics of the classic hymn by the English Poet and clergyman, John

Newton (1725 – 1805) titled "Amazing Grace." What a message of forgiveness is expressed in that hymn, declaring that our souls can be saved from despair and forgiveness is available through the mercy of God. Barnabas was known as the disciple of grace because of the relationship he had with the other disciples, and Peter actually admonished us in 2 Peter 3:18 that we should endeavor to "grow in grace."

This book is a great resource on the topic of grace, and as you read it, may you grow in grace concerning the assignment God has called you to carry out, and in your dealings with one another. May the Lord we serve transform us to become true disciples of His amazing grace, in Jesus name, Amen.

Pastor James Fadele
Chairman, RCCG NA Board of Coordinators

∽ Introduction ∽

---

*I do not at all understand the
mystery of grace –
only that it meets us where we are
but does not leave us where it found us.*

- Anne Lamott -

As a youth in West Africa, I saw many people around me excel and experience abundance amidst poverty and suffering. Many years ago, I was at an event that I should not have attended. I was upset because my mentor and friend was not there. The event was boring to me because it was worldly with many activities that are against my beliefs. It got me thinking – what was the unique virtue in my friend's life that placed him at the right place and at the right time? I asked myself the following questions over and over:

✓ **What keeps a minister rising?**

✓ **What makes a person's life better?**

✓ **What keeps a person healthy, refreshing and admirable?**

✓ **What wins souls?**

✓ **What brings multiplication?**

✓ **What brings fulfillment in life?**

✓ **What makes the race easy and exciting?**

✓ **What makes you finish the race well?**

✓ **What can turn a beggar into a celebrity?**

I discovered the power that makes the difference in life and that power is not association. Wrong connections can orchestrate or derail destiny, and Proverbs 13:20 MSG says, "Become wise by walking with the wise; hang out with fools and watch your life fall to pieces." Association can decide one's improvement or failure and "bad company corrupts good character" (1 Corinthians 15:33 NIV).

What is *The Highest Common Factor*?

It is not position or status. If you are in the right position and cannot express yourself, your life may slip downhill.

It is not money. Money cannot solve life's biggest problems. Money can make a man miserable. Some people have died prematurely and in some cases, committed suicide when they possessed sudden riches. Money can fly away without notice.

It is not location. If you settle in the wrong location, you may regret it. Lot chose a wrong location. "Lot looked up and saw that the whole plain of the Jordan was well watered, like the garden of the LORD, like the land of Egypt, toward Zoar. (This was before the LORD destroyed Sodom and Gomorrah.) So Lot chose for himself the whole plain of the Jordan and set out toward the east" (Genesis 13:10-11 NIV). As a result, he was displaced, relocated, lost his possessions, friends, and even his wife (Genesis 19:22-26). Do not move to a place without divine direction.

It is not education. I am not saying education is not important but many educated people are ignorant and have been corrupted through the wisdom of this world.

The Highest Common Factor is grace and it is often misconstrued. To classify grace as formulaic or essentially a mathematical logic would be naive. I am merely showing you a way to understand this enigmatic yet transformational phenomenon. In mathematics, the Highest Common Factor (H.C.F) for a set of numbers is the largest whole number that divides the set of numbers without any remainder. It is used mostly in expressing a set of fractions in their lowest term because the common factor can be easily cancelled out. For example, the factors of 4 are 1, 2 and 4 while the factors of 8 are 1, 2, 4 and 8. If you look at the factors of 4 and 8, the highest common factor is 4.

Abraham, Jacob, Joseph, Moses, Joshua - all these patriarchs had one common factor for success in their ministries and it was *the grace of God*. Of all the multiple integers of life listed above namely: position or status, money or purse power, location or opportunity, and education or knowledge; grace is the highest common integer that can cancel out the comparative advantage that any of them portend in a person's life. Grace is the largest factor that can divide through any issue in life without a remainder. Even more importantly, grace is commonly applied to all by faith because it is unmerited, unearned, undeserved, and the imparted work of Christ. It is the highest common factor in the lives of believers. Grace was paid for at Calvary and the currency was the precious blood of Jesus Christ. Although the wages of sin is death (eternal separation from the Father), grace makes a way for all Christians regardless of their stations in life.

To succeed in life, we need God's grace. Grace makes the difference in us. The Greek word for grace is *charis*, which means goodwill or God's kindness. Grace is God's sufficiency or God's fullness in the life of the believer. God told Paul, "My grace is sufficient for you, for my power is made perfect in weakness" (2 Corinthians 12:9 NIV). Grace is God's voluntary and loving favor given to us. No religious or moral effort can increase it because it comes only from God's mercy and love.

Grace is synonymous with mercy. In Hebrew, mercy (also kindness) is *chesed*, translated as God's enduring love. Mercy is God's undeserving pardon given to a sinner. Romans 6:23 says, "The wages of sin is death" so when one sins, one deserves to be punished, but for the grace of God which averts man's punishment. With grace in your life, all obstacles and limitations are removed from your life. The grace of God is inexhaustible and it covers everything and nothing can be added to it. God's grace account cannot be overdrawn because it is never-ending.

Grace provides answers to life's questions and brings spiritual blessings and breakthroughs. It makes man a leader. It places man at the right place and at the right time. With grace, you will not miss your hour of divine visitation. Grace puts you in front and not behind. A man of grace cannot be silenced or ignored. Anything you receive from the throne of grace cannot be taken away by anybody. Without grace, life is fruitless and powerless. When grace was missing in King Saul's life, he envied David and purposed to kill him (1 Samuel 18:8,12). A man of grace can go somewhere from nowhere and enjoy surplus in the midst of economic recession.

The greatest help, blessing or gift one can receive is grace and it sets us apart. In my high school days, my friend Yomi excelled in everything. He was admirable, very witty, a chorister, and a fine footballer. God's grace was evident in his life and I wanted it badly. I entered into a covenant relationship with the Lord, longed for Him and promised to serve Him. Grace, *The Highest Common Factor* is much needed in our lives. Do you know that the last note in the Bible is about the grace (Revelations 22:21)? Read this book and discover the true meaning of God's grace, its role in our lives, why we need it and how to get it.

Let us therefore come boldly to the throne of grace that we may obtain mercy and find grace to help in time of need.

Hebrews 4:16

∼1∼
GRACE is a *Certain* Beginning

Grace is a certain beginning of glory in us.

- Saint Thomas Aquinas -

The grace of God helps us start all over. Sometime ago I met Amy, a mother of three in her mid-thirties. Her adoptive father sexually assaulted her and consequently she left home at the age of 15, lived in more than ten cities and embraced different religions. Her past taunted her and brought on confusion in her life. She was so depressed that she became suicidal. She questioned God and searched for answers from place to place. In her own words, she says:

My mother is narcissistic and does not care whether I talk to her, and my dad has been in prison for over 10 years for murder. I try to live as stress-free as possible, but I would be lying if I said none of it bothered me. My sole concentration is on my family, their health, and getting out of debt. I want my boys to feel secure, stable, level-headed and confident. I don't know what the future holds, but I will be ready. Every time I try to get deeper into faith, something pulls me out. It's been happening for years.

Today, Amy has decided to put her past behind her and has invited our local church to come and start a Bible study in her house. She sees the power of God in her life, and is eager to hear God's word and receive grace for a fresh start. When grace is on you, all things fall in place. 2 Corinthians 5:17 says: "Therefore, if anyone *is* in Christ, *he is* a new creation; old things have passed away; behold, all things have become new."

God loves to give us a fresh start always. A fresh start is an opportunity given to us by God to start all over. God's grace changes situations and not men. God's grace is powerful and our abilities cannot match what grace can accomplish. You can start afresh with God regardless of age, your past, race, class or status. To start afresh, you must forget the past. Isaiah 43:18-19 teaches us that the past is always a burden and can rob us of our future. Any thought that brings regret can entangle us and hinder the new things God is about to release into our lives. Dwelling in the past triggers emotions that create moroseness, sadness and depression. The load becomes heavy, pins down the carrier and prevents him or her from moving forward. The past is a weight that lies in our way of progress and if we don't put it behind, we stumble and fall repeatedly. Living in the past prevents us from enjoying today.

Moses Started Over

Moses committed murder because he was blinded by his rage. Rashness, fury and anger clouded his judgment. Exodus 2:11-12 NCV says, "Moses grew and became a man. One day he visited his people and saw that they were forced to work very hard. He saw an Egyptian beating a Hebrew man, one of Moses' own people. Moses looked all around and saw that no one was watching, so he killed the Egyptian and hid his body in the sand." However, God's grace located Moses and he was sent out of Egypt to deliver his people. Moses felt inadequate and told God about his history of poor judgment and murder. He said: "Who *am* I that I should go to Pharaoh, and that I should bring the children of Israel out of Egypt?" (Exodus 3:11) He told God he was not right for the assignment.

Before a man can work for God, grace must first be extended to him. God released His grace on Moses and made him right and relevant for the assignment. He was delivered from low self-esteem and the "I cannot do it" mentality. God's grace removed the preferences and prejudices from Moses and he was anointed and his past was not an issue. By His grace, resources will abound in your life in Jesus name. In the throne room of grace, your past is forgotten by God.

The Israelites Enjoyed a Fresh Start

The Lord granted the Israelites a fresh start through grace released at Passover. Through Passover, God put an end to servitude and delivered the people from bondage. God gave them a fresh start. Like the people of Israel, you can begin again. "This month *shall be* your beginning of months; it *shall be* the first month of the year to you" (Exodus 12:2).

God Ignores Your Past

A man who could easily have been affected (or hindered) by his past was Apostle Paul. He was born an Israelite from the tribe of Benjamin; a strict and devout adherent to God's law. He took pride in his place of birth and education. He later became a persecutor of the church of Christ and even a murderer. However, God's grace was abundant in his life and his past was forgotten. He says in Philippians 3:13, "Brethren, *I do* not count myself to have apprehended; but one thing I do, forgetting those things which are behind and reaching forward to those things which are ahead."

God still releases grace for a fresh start. All you have to do is ask Him for a new life or a new beginning. In John 8:3-5, a woman was caught in adultery and brought to Jesus for His judgment. The grace of God was extended to her and she was given a fresh start. Her case was pathetic because the Law of Moses was against her. Her accusers were determined to destroy her, raging like voracious lions ready to devour their prey. They asked Jesus, "Teacher, this woman was caught in adultery, in the very act. Now Moses, in the law, commanded us that such should be stoned. But what do you say?" And Jesus answered in John 8:7-11 NCV:

"Anyone here who has never sinned can throw the first stone at her." Then Jesus bent over again and wrote on the ground. Those who heard Jesus began to leave one by one, first the older men and then the others. Jesus was left there alone with the woman standing before him. Jesus raised up again and asked her, "Woman, where are they? Has no one judged you guilty?" She answered, "No one, sir." Then Jesus said, "I also don't judge you guilty. You may go now, but don't sin anymore."

With long life I will satisfy him,
and show him my salvation.

❧ Psalm 91:16

∽ 2 ᗡ
GRACE is Long Life

When grace is joined with wrinkles, it is adorable.
There is an unspeakable dawn in happy old age.

- Victor Hugo -

Grace makes you cheat death. *The Brugada Syndrome* is a genetic disease that is characterized by abnormal electrocardiogram (ECG) findings and an increased risk of sudden cardiac death. It is also known as *Sudden Unexpected Death Syndrome (SUDS),* and is the most common cause of sudden death in young men without any known underlying cardiac disease. Brugada Syndrome causes sudden death by causing ventricular fibrillation (a deadly arrhythmia) in the heart.

On a fine Sunday afternoon, my friend Smith, a 49-year old statistician fainted during a visit to a friend's house. After his resuscitation at the hospital, his condition was diagnosed as Brugada Syndrome. God's grace for long life was extended to this fine Christian gentleman who is very active in his local church and faithful in organizing and keeping the church accounts. Grace located my friend and he was spared of an untimely death. Even though he fainted, the grace of God revived him and made him aware of his condition. The generational curse of sudden or premature death in his family has been broken. Many people have died due to SUDS but with God's grace, we cheat death.

God's Grace upon Abraham

God showered his grace on Abraham and gave him long life. He was blessed in all things (Genesis 24:1). He enjoyed life to the fullest, fulfilled his earnest heart desires and did not have any regrets. "Abraham lived for 175 years, and he died at a ripe old age, having lived a long and satisfying life. He breathed his last and joined his ancestors in death" (Genesis 25:7-8 NLT).

Jacob Enjoyed Grace

Jacob lived well and enjoyed grace. Although Jacob made mistakes in raising his kids but the grace of God upon him brought the family together. He ran away from home and became a fugitive in a strange land, fell into the hand of a trickster uncle and ended up marrying two sisters. Through it all, grace made him an overcomer.

Jacob had 12 sons and one was sold into slavery. Eventually he was reconciled to his supposedly dead son Joseph. Imagine the joy he felt at his old age when he saw Joseph again. He ended up living and feasting in the best part of Egypt even in a time of great famine. Genesis 47:11-12 says "Joseph situated his father and his brothers, and gave them a possession in the land of Egypt, in the best of the land, in the land of Ramses, as Pharaoh had commanded. Then Joseph provided his father, his brothers, and his entire father's household with bread, according to the number in *their* families."

Jacob's life was rough but grace made it smooth. God's grace upon Jacob made years of hard labor seem like days. Jacob described his life in an intriguing manner in Genesis 47:7-9:

"Pharaoh said to Jacob, "How old are you?" And Jacob said to Pharaoh, "The days of the years of my pilgrimage are one hundred and thirty years; few and evil have been the days of the years of my life, and they have not attained to the days of the years of the life of my fathers' in the days of their pilgrimage."

Jacob saw his children's children before he died and even blessed them. The grace of God upon him allowed him to die in peace and not in pain and was able to tell his children where he wanted to be buried. Genesis 49:33 says, "And when Jacob had finished commanding his sons, he drew his feet up into the bed and breathed his last, and was gathered to his people." Even Balaam desired the kind of life and death that Jacob experienced. He described Jacob's death in Numbers 23:10 by saying: "Who can count the dust of Jacob, or number one-fourth of Israel? Let me die the death of the righteous, and let my end be like his!"

The Divine Grace upon Moses

The same grace to live long was upon Moses. He was born (Exodus 2:1-10) at a time Pharaoh was killing Hebrew male children. His mother saw God's grace and beauty on him and hid him for three months until she couldn't do it anymore. Then, she put him in a basket and placed him among the reeds along the bank of the Nile River. God's grace intervened and placed Moses in the hands of Pharaoh's daughter. She had compassion for him, got a nanny (the child's natural birth mother) to nurse him.

God's grace was with Moses even during his stay at Pharaoh's palace, as a wanderer in the desert and while leading about two million stiff-necked people through the wilderness. Grace confirmed God's words in his life with signs and wonders. Psalm 105:37 MSG says "He led Israel out, their arms filled with loot, and not one among his tribes even stumbled."

In his old age, Moses was strong and healthy. He had sound mind and great memory. The grace of God upon him preserved his organs, systems, cells and tissues without any form of degenerative changes. Deuteronomy 34:7 says, "Moses was one hundred and twenty years old when he died. His eyes were not dim nor his natural vigor diminished."

Is there a secret to long life? What makes a person live above the life expectancy of his area? Science has researched and still researching the secrets of longevity. Many anti-aging suggestions have cropped up. No doubt, genetics, access to health care, hygiene, nutrition, exercise and crime rates affect life expectancy. I had a conversation with Thomas recently. He has been on this earth for nearly 100 years. He is in great physical shape with good mobility and functional ability and doesn't use walking aid. He has lived an interesting life. He relocated to Canada from England in 1948 after fighting for seven years in the world war. Thomas lives alone, worked until the age of 65 and volunteered until the age of 97. He has devoted his life to humanity and has looked after different people at their dying moments. He is hardworking, caring and very smart. He knows my children's names and ages, great with numbers and does not need a calendar for his appointments. God's grace preserved his life in his army days and continues to do so to this day.

God releases grace as He pleases. Even though grace prolongs life, some martyrs of the faith have died young. Robert Murray M'Cheyne, one of the godliest pastors in the history of the church died at the age of 29 years. Many other godly men and women died young. A Christian lifestyle will generally be healthier and probably statistics would show that on average Christians live longer. Sometimes when our work and purpose is done on earth, the Lord is pleased to take His children home at a time that seems too soon for us but is indeed perfect because it is God's time. Grace is not a matter of earth days, it is eternal. It is much greater than human sense of time. Grace makes us more than the shell of our bodies!

For by grace you have been
saved through faith,
and that not of yourselves;
it is the gift of God.

🌿 Ephesians 2:8

~ 3 ~
GRACE Loves
the Unlovable

*Grace is the love that gives,
that loves the unlovely and the unlovable.*

- Oswald C. Hoffmann -

Today's world is filled with unforgiveness and a desire to seek revenge. God loves us and grants us undeserved second chance. We are His children and carry His DNA and we are expected to forgive and love. Forgiveness is the only option for Christians (Matthew 6:14). In Luke 15, people came to hear Jesus but the Pharisees and religious scholars were not pleased. They murmured and complained that Jesus received sinners and ate with them. In response to their fault-finding attitude, Jesus shared the parable of the prodigal son to show us the way God loves us.

In this parable, the younger son asks his father to give him the portion of the inheritance due to him. In

Jewish culture, the eldest son always takes a double portion of the inheritance simply for posterity because he is obligated to preserve the family name. The father granted the younger son's request and gave him his inheritance. This boy left for a far country, lived wildly and squandered everything. I call this a spirit of wastefulness. His condition was made worse by an economic downturn or recession which pervaded that country. He was poor and hungry so he got a job feeding pigs. This is quite degrading in Jewish custom because pigs are considered unclean (Leviticus 11:7). He left home as a son, free and rich, but the way of sin changed him to a servant, bound and poor. Sin takes away your liberty and joy.

Eventually he came to his senses and did a self-evaluation. To make quality decisions, we must question the status quo. All great scientists have questioned the status quo. Don't accept your condition. If you cannot change what you are comfortable with, then change the things you despise. Frequent self-evaluations are necessary and we must ask ourselves these questions:

>> **Why am I in this condition?**
>> **Is this my best?**
>> **Where was I last year?**
>> **What has happened to me?**
>> **Why did it happen to me?**

The young son decided to go home. His father was overjoyed when he saw him, "his heart pounding, he ran out, embraced him and kissed him" (Luke 15:20 MSG). His father celebrated his return, summoned his servants to bring out the best robe for him (a sign of distinction and honor), put sandals on his feet (a symbol of freedom, because slaves at that time were barefoot), put a ring on his finger (symbolic of power and authority) and killed the best calf. His father's joy is similar to the "joy in heaven over one sinner who changes his heart and life" (Luke 15:7 NCV).

The story took another turn when the older brother returned home from the field. He wondered what the celebration was all about. He refused to go inside when he learnt his father was celebrating the return of his wasteful younger brother. This shows that the older brother was just as lost as the prodigal son. He was legalistic. Legalism is as much sin as adultery and rebellion. Condemning your brother or looking down on others is legalism. Legalism is a spirit that will not allow the movement of God. It is a spirit that criticizes others. Legalism is one of Satan's tools to distract the church. The devil is the accuser of the brethren. Legalism consists of man-made rules and you cannot be saved by man-made rules but only by grace.

The older brother wanted to have revenge but the father wanted to restore. God's grace is so powerful that what man cannot do in many years, His grace will do in a few seconds. The elder brother syndrome is present in today's church and it has made some Christians forget the grace of God and opt for man-made rules. It makes them pursue discipline, devotion, self-righteousness, fulfillment of law over the grace of God. Through grace, we enjoy forgiveness that we are unqualified to receive. Grace transcends personal abilities and divinely elevates man.

The father represents our heavenly Father, the prodigal son represents the penitent sinner and the elder brother reflects the attitude of self-righteous Christians. Our God is a God of love and desires to bring all His children together. John 3:16-17 says: "For God so loved the world that He gave His only begotten Son, that whoever believes in Him should not perish but have everlasting life. For God did not send His Son into the world to condemn the world, but that the world through Him might be saved."

Many *are* the afflictions of the righteous;
but the LORD delivers him out of them all.

❧ Psalms 34:19

4

GRACE Overcomes Afflictions

Whole, unbruised, unbroken men are of little use to God.

- J.R. Miller -

Before God can use a man greatly, He must wound him deeply.

- A.W. Tozer -

According to Webster's dictionary, affliction is "something that causes persistent pain, distress, great suffering or ill health." Affliction is synonymous with hardship, adversity, misery, torment and tribulation. Affliction is part of life and no one is exempt from it. Whether we like it or not, we will experience affliction. Job 5:7 says, "Yet man is born to trouble as the sparks fly upward." Many afflictions are unexpected or unplanned but what we need in the time of affliction is grace to help us endure to the end. We should not allow the pains and pressures of afflictions to derail us from our God-given assignment. Affliction can either make us bitter or better.

God always releases grace to overcome affliction. In the midst of afflictions, one is not alone. God's Word in Hebrews 13:5 says, "For He Himself has said, *"I will never leave you nor forsake you."* Challenges are part of life and they make us stronger. Affliction changes the way we think, reason and speak. It makes us focus on God and not ourselves. When Paul was passing through afflictions, he prayed to God to remove them, but God showed up and reminded him of the grace to overcome affliction that was in his life. Paul says in 2 Corinthians 12:7-9 NIV::

> "To keep me from becoming conceited because of these surpassingly great revelations, there was given me a thorn in my flesh, a messenger of Satan, to torment me. Three times I pleaded with the Lord to take it away from me. But he said to me, "My grace is sufficient for you, for my power is made perfect in weakness."

I have been able to pray more, review and examine my life in the midst of afflictions. If not for afflictions, many of my God-given gifts would have remained inactive. Not too long ago, an evil propaganda was started to bring me and family down in our ministerial work. It was so terrible and disheartening that it caused us heartache and many sleepless nights. Many people were hungry to hear bad news about us. We cried, prayed and constantly encouraged ourselves. It was during this crisis that our daughter suddenly became sick. We recognized the devil's attack and prayed earnestly for grace at that hour of our need. We even asked a general overseer of a ministry who was visiting our city to stay with us as a seed to overcome the spiritual warfare. He stayed and prayed with us.

Her sickness was sudden and she was rushed to the hospital. Even at the hospital, the devil was still at work because we waited for more than four hours for a three minute consultation with the emergency room doctor. The sickness lingered and she was eventually transferred to a bigger hospital about an hour away from us. We were informed that she needed to undergo an urgent specialized investigation. My wife and I felt as if all hell would break loose and the pressure and burden on us was indescribable.

I needed someone's shoulder to cry on and I called a relative who had experienced a similar situation. He spoke into my spirit and said, "The God of grace you serve faithfully will not disappoint you." Eventually the medical results came and we were told she needed an urgent surgery. We were so afraid but grace sustained her and she came out of the surgery whole without any complications. Her pediatrician saw her a few weeks later and exclaimed, "thank God you are still with us; this was a near-death miss. It's a miracle!" Isn't God's grace wonderful?

Grace makes every sweat sweet and turns every affliction to affection from our loving Father. God's grace makes you not use your challenges and afflictions as an excuse but a springboard for promotion. Afflictions move us forward. Leviticus 26:21 says that if you refuse to listen and learn during afflictions, they will multiply. Grace during affliction removes complaints, whining, doubts, and false perspectives. Paul never looked back or doubted God's to sustain him and he was ready to suffer for the sake of the gospel. Grace is the invisible power that helped Paul overcome the pressure, pains and disappointments of ministerial work. The grace of God was so mighty on him that he was neither demoralized nor disappointed in the race of life.

Take a look at Philip. He was built up in crisis (Acts 8:8). As a result of persecution, he went to Samaria; single-handedly brought joy to a whole city and fulfilled his mission on earth. In times of affliction, pray (James 5:13) for grace to overcome the affliction. 2 Corinthians 4:8-11 says:

> "We are hard-pressed on every side, yet not crushed; we are perplexed, but not in despair; persecuted, but not forsaken; struck down, but not destroyed always carrying about in the body the dying of the Lord Jesus, that the life of Jesus also may be manifested in our body. For we who live are always delivered to death for Jesus' sake, that the life of Jesus also may be manifested in our mortal flesh."

But You, O LORD, *are* a shield for me,
My glory and the One who lifts
up my head.

❦ Psalms 3:3

∼ 5 ∼

God's GRACE
Helps Us Excel

It is a wretched taste to be gratified with mediocrity when the excellent lies before us.

- Isaac D'Israel -

Excellence is the ability to stand out and go beyond or surpass in good qualities or laudable deeds. God's grace of excellence was upon Daniel even when he was in his home country because Daniel was one of the best youth that the king of Babylon selected. Daniel 1:3-4 NIV says:

> "Then the king ordered Ashpenaz, chief of his court officials, to bring in some of the Israelites from the royal family and the nobility - young men without any physical defect, handsome, showing aptitude for every kind of learning, well informed, quick

to understand, and qualified to serve in the king's palace. He was to teach them the language and literature of the Babylonians."

In the strange land of Babylon, these young men were assigned a daily amount of food and wine from the king's table but Daniel rejected the king's delicacies because he did not want to defile himself. The grace of excellence was more evident in him when king's chief of staff allowed him to eat vegetables alone instead of the king's delicacy. "Daniel and his three friends looked healthier and better nourished than the young men who had been eating the food assigned by the king" (Daniel 1:15).

Daniel was not controlled by his circumstances and overcame the plot of man. His faith did not waver; he maintained his integrity and gave himself to prayer. He was wise, intelligent and smart. When the king of Babylon had a dream and nobody could interpret it, Daniel's skills were sought out (Daniel 5:13-15). Daniel interpreted the king's dreams and was promoted to the position of a prime minister in this foreign land.

God's grace makes a man unstoppable, unquenchable, unmovable, untouchable and unreachable by the enemy.

Joseph was another man with excellent spirit. Although he was hated by his siblings, thrown into a pit and sold as a slave, God used this affliction to prepare him for his future promotion. "The LORD was with Joseph, so he succeeded in everything he did as he served in the home of his Egyptian master. Potiphar noticed this and realized that the LORD was with Joseph, giving him success in everything he did" (Genesis 39:2-3 NLT). Potiphar's wife desired Joseph because he was a very handsome and well-built young man but he rejected her advances. He was eventually thrown into prison for an offense he did not commit but God was working out His purposes for Joseph.

Sometimes God allows us to be in nasty circumstances to promote us. Romans 8:28 says: "And we know that all things work together for good to those who love God, to those who are the called according to His purpose." God's grace was upon Joseph and helped him resist temptation. Joseph pleased God and was connected to the king's butler and baker. The favor of God was upon him and he interpreted their dreams. The excellent spirit of God in Joseph enabled him to correctly interpret the king's dreams. As a result, he was promoted to the position of a prime minister (Genesis 41:37-41). Joseph went from the pit to Potiphar's house, and then on to prison and eventually catapulted to the king's presence.

Excellence overrides limitations and God will elevate you regardless of race, accent or nationality. The grace of excellence does not exonerate us from hard work. The onus still rests on us to be diligent in our pursuits with careful preparation and planning. The preparation can be in the form of prayer, studying, working hard, ensuring instructions are followed, openness to new ideas, modifying or changing lifestyles, enrolling in schools, writing tests or examinations. Be careful not to disrupt the grace of God in your life through carelessness and laziness. Paul emphasized the importance of hard work in 1 Corinthians 15:9-10 NIV:

> "For I am the least of the apostles and do not even deserve to be called an apostle, because I persecuted the church of God. But by the grace of God I am what I am, and his grace to me was not without effect. No, I worked harder than all of them—yet not I, but the grace of God that was with me."

Paul enjoyed the abundance of God's grace and excelled in ministry. Take a look at Jotham's life in 2 Chronicles 27:6. In the midst of atrocities and corruption, he purposed to please God and he later excelled. He "became mighty, because he prepared his ways before the LORD his God." There is no substitute for obedience. Obey the governing laws of God and you will succeed in life.

I recently had an interesting discussion with a friend, an Obstetrician and Gynecologist, who by the grace of God has excelled against all odds especially in places where women are treated as second-class citizens. Her nickname is *the record breaker*. In her testimony she says:

I finished my residency in record time because of the grace of God upon my life and I did not re-sit any of my exams. Re-writing exams was very popular at the time because medical school is very intensive. Women were mostly affected because of the responsibilities of being wives and mothers. In my situation, I was also a Christian worker and money was limited. I had to balance my life and not collapse. My success was by the grace of God and nothing else. Out of six residents in my group that took a particular exam, I was the only one that passed. I was very humbled when one of the senior residents asked me for advice on how to pass exams. I knew that God's grace to excel was upon me. To God be the glory, she took my advice and passed.

The hands of Zerubbabel have laid the foundation of this temple; his hands shall also finish *it*. Then you will know that the LORD of hosts has sent me to you.

🌱 Zechariah 4:9

～ 6 ～
God's GRACE Helps
Us Finish Well

---

*There are two kinds of people,
those who finish what they start and so on.*

- Robert Byrne -

God finishes everything He begins. When God stepped into the world, the earth was without form and void and darkness covered the deep waters (Genesis 1:1-2). God started the great work of creation and finished it on the sixth day. God is a great Finisher. Philippians 1:6 says, "Being confident of this very thing, that He who has begun a good work in you will complete it until the day of Jesus Christ."

Every human being is on this earth for a purpose or an assignment but only a few finish their assignments. Some start well with good intentions, high aspirations, confidence and vigor but never finish well. There are many starters or beginners but very few achievers and finishers. Are you going to finish what you were born to finish? God is not a God of unfinished things but a God of completion. We were created in the image of God and have the breath of God, so we must complete what we were born to do on earth. Anything we start and terminate along the way is called *spiritual abortion*. When Jesus Christ was on earth he knew His assignment (John 4:34) and He finished well (John 19:30). God still releases grace to finish well.

A man of grace looks for ways
to turn every negative situation
into a positive one.

Paul is also an example of a finisher (2 Timothy 4:7). Paul remembered the grace that granted him personal revelation and emboldened him to not compromise God's word. Paul had grace that turned a persecutor into an apostle. He enjoyed grace to overcome warfare. He had several near-misses in his life but the grace of God kept him. Paul experienced:

✓ **Grace to live above the struggles of ministry,**

✓ **Grace that removed barriers, inhibitions and limitations from his path.**

✓ **Grace that moved him forward through the valleys of the shadow of death.**

✓ Grace that supplied all of his needs according to His riches in Christ Jesus.

✓ Grace that gave him energy, stamina, capacity and strengthened him to do all things.

✓ Grace that removed the *I cannot do it mentality* and replaced it with the desire to do God's will.

✓ Grace that rescued him from destruction and equipped him for service.

✓ Grace that brought miracles to his ministry.

Another finisher was Nehemiah. He discovered his mission on earth by speaking to remnants from his country while he was in a foreign land. When he heard that the city walls of his country were broken, he sat down and wept, mourned and fasted and prayed to the God of heaven (Nehemiah 1). He saw an opportunity to fulfill his purpose and sought grace from heaven. In difficult situations, grace will make a man look to heaven and cry out to God.

God's grace keeps
you focused.

Nehemiah was the king's cup bearer and was responsible for tasting the king's food and drink to make sure it was not poisoned. He had immediate access to the king. He prayed for favor in the sight of the king and God answered his prayers. The king favored him and Nehemiah set out on the journey of rebuilding the walls of Jerusalem. The tasks were huge but God's grace uplifted him. The distractions were many but God's grace kept him focused. Those with oppositions were determined to stop him at all costs but God's grace made him overcome all. Nehemiah was condemned, criticized, intimidated, bullied, mocked, despised, and laughed at by the enemies of progress but God's grace helped him to the finishing line. The grace of God on Nehemiah made him finish the rebuilding of the broken walls of Jerusalem in grand style!

You can recognize your assignment and finish it if you will cry to God for grace. Will you do that today?

It is more blessed to give
than to receive.

❧ **Acts 20:35**

⁓ 7 ⁓

By God's GRACE, We Give

*For grace is given not because we
have done good works,
but in order that we may be able to do them.*

- Saint Augustine of Hippo -

Giving does not always involve money. You can give time, talents or treasures. Giving is a principle of God through which increase comes into our lives. It is a prerequisite to fruitfulness. One of the governing laws God released at creation is the principle of sowing precious seeds and reaping (Genesis 1:29). A seed is anything that has the potential to become more and everyone has seeds to offer. It is a seed that is released or given away that is saved, the one kept is lost. Genesis 8:22 NIV says, "As long as the earth endures, seedtime and harvest, cold and heat, summer and winter, day and night will never cease." In other words, as long as this planet earth remains, the law of sowing and reaping will never fail. Our God demonstrated this grace by giving His only begotten Son to save mankind from sin. As a result of that precious gift, the hope of eternity has been delivered to mankind.

Some years ago, a group of pastors and I shared some ministry experiences and I said that "giving is by grace." Apparently that statement did not go well with them. My statement is true because if one experiences the grace to give, giving will flow naturally and he or she will no longer depend on his or her financial status. Such people give whether they are rich or poor. In Mark 12:43-44 MSG, Jesus observed the way they gave in the temple and singled out the gift of a poor widow. "Jesus called his disciples over and said, 'The truth is that this poor widow gave more to the collection than all the others put together. All the others gave what they'll never miss; she gave extravagantly what she couldn't afford—she gave her all."

Examples of *Serious* Givers

Abraham gave his son Isaac as instructed by God and God released new blessings to him. Genesis 22:15-18 NIV says:

> "The angel of the LORD called to Abraham from heaven a second time and said, 'I swear by myself, declares the LORD, that because you have done this

and have not withheld your son, your only son, I will surely bless you and make your descendants as numerous as the stars in the sky and as the sand on the seashore. Your descendants will take possession of the cities of their enemies, and through your offspring all nations on earth will be blessed, because you have obeyed me."

Ruth gave herself to her mother-in law, and she was rewarded with an eternal blessing. Ruth was a widow in a strange land and after the death of her husband, her mother-in-law told her two daughters-in-law (Ruth and Orpah); "Return home, my daughters" (Ruth 1:11 NIV). Orpah left but the grace of giving upon Ruth made her release herself to Naomi without any strings attached.

Ruth 1:16-18 NIV
"But Ruth replied, "Don't urge me to leave you or to turn back from you. Where you go I will go, and where you stay I will stay. Your people will be my people and your God my God. Where you die I will die, and there I will be buried. May the LORD deal with me, be it ever so severely, if anything but death separates you and me." When Naomi realized that Ruth was determined to go with her, she stopped urging her."'

This grace of giving upon Ruth brought her favor, blessings and increase. It took away shame and disgrace. Ruth remarried and brought forth a son whose lineage brought forth our Lord and Savior Jesus Christ (Matthew 1:1,5).

The Macedonian Church was rich in the grace of giving. The church members were in extreme poverty and yet they gave willingly. They even pleaded to give to the work of God. The grace of giving made them beg Paul to take their offering so that they would have the privilege of giving. People with the grace of giving are always looking for the right soil to sow seeds. They do not allow the season of sowing slip by them because they know that sowing the right quantity in the right season produces a great harvest. They are eager to continue with the cycle of giving and receiving regardless of their circumstances.

> 2 Corinthians 8:1-4 NIV
> "And now, brothers, we want you to know about the grace that God has given the Macedonian churches. Out of the most severe trial, their overflowing joy and their extreme poverty welled up in rich generosity. For I testify that they gave as much as they were able, and even beyond their ability. Entirely on their own, they urgently pleaded with us for the privilege of sharing in this service to the saints."

An example of a great giver in our contemporary world was John D. Rockefeller. He lived a life of giving and established a foundation that has been changing people's lives up till today. His life of giving might have contributed to his miraculous healing of a strange disease in his early fifties and he lived up to ninety-eight years. Grace will ensure that you do not faint in sowing perpetually.

For the mountains shall depart
and the hills be removed,
but My kindness shall not depart from you,
nor shall My covenant of
peace be removed,"
says the LORD, who has mercy on you.

❦ Isaiah 54:10

8

God's GRACE Straightens Night Seasons

---

*Grace isn't a little prayer
you chant before receiving a meal.
It's a way to live.
The law tells me how crooked I am.
Grace comes along and straightens me out.*

- D.L Moody -

Night season is a period in one's life where he or she experiences gloominess, hopelessness or loneliness. In such situations detours occur. If they are crooked, God's grace will straighten them out. Paul had some detours in his ministerial journey (Acts 16:1-8) and some night seasons. In Acts 16:9-10 MSG:

"Paul had a dream: A Macedonian stood on the far shore and called across the sea, "Come over to Macedonia and help us!" The dream gave Paul his map. We went to work at once getting things ready to cross over to Macedonia. All the pieces had come together. We knew now for sure that God had called us to preach the good news to the Europeans."

We go through night seasons for one reason or another. People are kept awake at night especially if important decisions are to be made. Decision-making can be very challenging due to hectic schedules in today's world. Some people are kept awake at night before and during examinations. In my medical school days in Nigeria, it was very tough to burn the midnight oil daily. While students in other disciplines were on vacation, we were on campus studying and working extra hard.

A few years ago, during a conversation with an old classmate, he mentioned that if we had known what we know now, we would have used some of our time in medical school to do meaningful things.

Some people are kept awake at night by pornography especially with today's Internet access. Others are kept awake at night with alcohol and partying. A lot are following the footsteps of King Belshazzar of Babylon. His night of dining and wining (Daniel 5:1-4) was turned to a night of distress and death (Daniel 5:5-31).

What do you do in your night season?

Paul and Silas praised God and prayed in their midnight hour and God showered them with grace to overcome their enemies (Acts 16). Luke 6:12 says that Jesus "went out to a mountainside to pray, and spent the night praying to God." Isaac equally used his night seasons to pray and praise God. Even in his success, he turned to God. He was not too big and busy to commune with God. He found time to worship his Maker and God visited him in night seasons and made a covenant of blessings which surpassed his previous blessings. God released him into a higher level of prosperity and he was later celebrated by the people who ignored and antagonized him.

Genesis 26:22-25 NLT
"Abandoning that one, Isaac moved on and dug another well. This time there was no dispute over it, so Isaac named the place Rehoboth (which means "open space"), for he said, "At last the LORD has created enough space for us to prosper in this land." From there Isaac moved to Beersheba, where the LORD appeared to him on the night of his arrival. "I am the God of your father, Abraham," he said. "Do not be afraid, for I am with you and will bless you. I will multiply your descendants, and they will become a great nation. I will do this because of my promise to Abraham, my servant." Then Isaac built an altar there and worshiped the LORD. He set up his camp at that place, and his servants dug another well."

Grace brings responsibility too because anyone God confers grace on is expected to be responsible. Isaac enjoyed grace from God. He was resourceful and lived a life of purpose. Isaac refused to live under the shadow of his father and channeled his own life. He enjoyed four-fold grace and he did not frustrate the grace of God on his life (Genesis 26:13). Isaac was controlled by faith. He had faith in God regardless of his circumstances. In the midst of famine, he wanted to leave the land of Gerar for Egypt but God warned him to remain there (Genesis 26:1-3).

A man of faith knows that every problem has a solution and every Goliath can be brought down with a small stone on a sling. A man of faith never gives up. A man controlled by faith never wastes time on non-essentials.

Faith makes you see what God has prepared for you. When you see what God has prepared for you, it will change the way you live. You will not complain and whine in the midst of challenges. What Isaac saw with his eyes of faith changed his focus about life and was ready to wait for the place God had prepared for him. Isaac sowed by faith in famine and experienced a hundredfold harvest.

Faith means believing and experiencing the impossible. He was able to dig a well in a period of prolonged dry season (Genesis 26:18-22). The enemies covered his wells and drove him out. However, because he was controlled by faith, he moved from one place to the other without complaining or fighting.

Every human being is controlled by one factor or another. Some are controlled by fear while others are controlled by faith. Absalom was controlled by lust for power. He sought for power to be king and in the end he died without realizing his dreams. Cain was controlled by anger, bitterness, hatred and envy. He ended up killing his brother and God placed a curse on him turning him to a fugitive.

What is controlling your life? Are you controlled by faith? Hebrews 12:2 NLT says, "we do this by keeping our eyes on Jesus, the champion who initiates and perfects our faith. Because of the joy awaiting him, he endured the cross, disregarding its shame. Now he is seated in the place of honor beside God's throne."

For the grace of God that brings salvation
has appeared to all men,
teaching us that, denying ungodliness
and worldly lusts,
we should live soberly, righteously, and
godly in the present age.

❧ Titus 2:11-12

The Power of Transferable GRACE

When grace is heavy on you, you will be envied. Before God could reveal things to Isaac, he was identified by God as a son of Abraham. Genesis 26:2-5 NLT says, "The LORD appeared to Isaac and said: "Do not go down to Egypt, but do as I tell you. Live here as a foreigner in this land, and I will be with you and bless you. I hereby confirm that I will give all these lands to you and your descendants, just as I solemnly promised Abraham, your father. I will cause your descendants to become as numerous as the stars of the sky, and I will give them all these lands. And through your descendants all the nations of the earth will be blessed. I will do this because Abraham listened to me and obeyed all my requirements, commands, decrees, and instructions.""

The Transferred Grace of a Father

In today's world, some people think if they have the Holy Spirit, they don't need spiritual fathers and live carelessly. A father provides spiritual covering. Everyone comes to this world as a result of the seed sown by a father. There are lots of fatherless Christians today. Some of these Christians wander around and struggle with a lot of issues of faith. There are some blessings that only a father can release into our lives.

In Acts 18:24-28, Apollos was described as a saved Jew who could mesmerize any audience with his oratory ability. He was zealous, articulate in the Scriptures and eager to teach the word of God. However, this man was sincerely wrong because he only knew the baptism of John. He had not been exposed to the ministry of reconciliation by grace. A couple named Aquila and Priscilla heard him one day and brought him to their house to teach him the total gospel. This shows there are many things we need to learn from our spiritual fathers and mothers. Apollos had a teachable spirit. He was open to the new teaching and revelations he did not know. As a result he was able to excel in his ministry and was of immense help to believers (Acts 18:27-28).

Why do we need spiritual fathers?

Fathers are alert to the conditions of their children and ensure they are brought up with sound training. Hebrews 12:5-8 NLT says:

> "My child, don't make light of the LORD's discipline, and don't give up when he corrects you. For the LORD disciplines those he loves, and he punishes each one he accepts as his child." As you endure this divine discipline, remember that God is treating you as his

own children. Who ever heard of a child who is never disciplined by its father? If God doesn't discipline you as he does all of his children, it means that you are illegitimate and are not really his children at all."

A father pronounces blessings. Even nations need fathers of faith they can go to in crisis. In 2 Kings 2:19-22, there was a national problem in Jericho and the leaders visited their spiritual father Elisha and asked him to pronounce blessings on their land to reverse the curse upon the land. Elisha did as they asked and addressed the source of the problem and the curse on the land was removed up to this date (2 Kings 2:20-21).

Barnabas was a father to Paul and he provided support and love to him. In Acts 9:26-27 NLT, "when Saul arrived in Jerusalem, he tried to meet with the believers, but they were all afraid of him. They did not believe he had truly become a believer! Then Barnabas brought him apostles and told them how Saul had seen the Lord on the way to Damascus and how the Lord had spoken to Saul. He also told them that Saul had preached boldly in the name of Jesus in Damascus."

People judged Paul based on his old reputation. He used to be a persecutor and became a preacher. The grace of God made him a new creature but people could not forget his past. His past became a stigma but Barnabas encouraged him and made him feel relevant. "Barnabas was good man, full of the Holy Spirit and strong in faith. And many people were brought to the Lord. Then Barnabas went on to Tarsus to look for Saul. When he found him, he brought him back to Antioch. Both of them stayed there with the church for a full year, teaching large crowds of people" (Acts 11:19-26 NLT).

However, negative attributes can also be transferred from a father to his child. Abraham's *lying syndrome* (Genesis 12:10-17) where he lied that his wife Sarah was his sister was transferred to Isaac (Genesis 26:7-11). Isaac also lied to the people of Philistines that his wife Rebecca was his sister. When confronted by Abimelech, the king of the Philistines, he said he was afraid.

The *spoilt child syndrome* was transferred from Eli to Samuel. Eli's children were wayward and disobedient and the same thing happened to Samuel (Eli's spiritual son). His children were corrupt and polluted the temple.

So, who is your spiritual father? Be careful of who you call your spiritual father so that negative attributes are not transferred to you. Let God connect you appropriately, so that He can work everything together for good as He did in the life of Isaac.

For the law was given through Moses,
but grace and truth came
through Jesus Christ.

❧ John 1:17

⌒ 10 ⌒

How to
Receive GRACE

*Grace is but glory begun,
and glory is but grace perfected.*

- Jonathan Edwards -

There is only one way to receive grace: be connected to God the Father, God the Son and God the Holy Spirit. The connection is through God's only begotten Son, Jesus Christ. You must have a relationship with Jesus. This relationship involves confessing your sins and inviting Jesus Christ into your life as your personal Lord and Savior. Jesus was sent by God to earth to reconcile the sinful man to God. Sin terminates the destiny of mankind but Jesus came to redeem man from destruction.

The connection with Jesus ensures the release of nourishments to our survival. One of the nourishments is grace. In John 15:5, Jesus says, "I am the vine, you *are* the branches. He who abides in Me, and I in him, bears much fruit; for without Me you can do nothing." This connection is like the growth of a bamboo tree. Bamboos are giant, fast-growing grasses with woody stems. Without branches, they look sluggish but as soon as the roots take hold, they can grow as fast as 48 inches in 24 hours. The growth of a bamboo tree cannot be controlled by cutting its canes. If you do that, the roots grow more.

When you are connected to Jesus Christ, you receive grace and more grace and His strength is exchanged for your weakness. God releases grace to grow and to multiply. The connection to God removes barriers. Once the connection with Jesus stops, we dry up just like the bamboo will dry up. In Philippians 4:13, Paul says, "I can do all things through Christ who strengthens me." This connection also entails being like Jesus who excelled in communion with the Father, character, conduct and service. Our world emphasizes civil liberty and people's human rights. Therefore, to be Christ like, we must give up our rights in God's service. Jesus gave up His rights in order to have maximum impact in this world. His service was sacrificial and selfless.

For the LORD God *is* a sun and shield;
the LORD will give grace and glory;
No good *thing* will He withhold
from those who walk uprightly.

✳ Psalm 84:11

～ 11 ～

How to Increase
in GRACE

---

*A state of mind that sees God in
everything is evidence of growth in grace
and a thankful heart.*

- Charles G. Finney -

God is a great giver and He is willing to release His
abundant grace on us. There are many ways to increase
in grace but in my years of studying the scriptures, I
found out four ways that guarantee increase of grace
from God. The early apostles moved from grace to great
grace in Acts 4:33 and these four qualities were evident
in their lives. A heart that yearns for more grace from
God must be ready to honor God, be humble, be holy
and give unceasing thanks to God.

To honor means to hold in high esteem, to treat with
reverence and respect. It is to value, to treat as precious

and weighty. God must be honored. God also expects a son to honor his father. A woman came to Jesus and poured precious ointment on Him. The Lord considered it as an honor, even though others questioned whether the money used to buy the ointment should have been given to the poor. We are expected to honor parents and those in position of authority like pastors or ministers of the Gospel. We honor them by holding them in high esteem, attending to their needs, supporting them and by giving gifts to them. Romans 13:7 NIV says, "give everyone what you owe him: If you owe taxes, pay taxes; if revenue, then revenue; if respect, then respect; if honor, then honor."

When you honor your parents (Ephesians 6:1-3), God releases grace to live long. Honor your father and mother—which is the first commandment with a promise— "that it may go well with you and that you may enjoy long life on the earth." If we disobey or dishonor our parents, it can bring curses to our lives. "If you insult your father or mother, your light will be snuffed out in total darkness" (Proverbs 20:20 NLT). Heaven also takes note of our honor and rewards us accordingly and God also honors those who honor Him (1 Samuel 2:30). Matthew 10:40-42 says:

> "He who receives you receives me, and he who receives me receives the one who sent me. Anyone who receives a prophet because he is a prophet will receive a prophet's reward, and anyone who receives a righteous man because he is a righteous man will receive a righteous man's reward. And if

anyone gives even a cup of cold water to one of these little ones because he is my disciple, I tell you the truth, he will certainly not lose his reward."

Humility is defined as the quality or condition of being humble. Pride is the opposite of humility and pride is man's attempt to rival God and I call it, exaggerated self esteem. Every human being has self esteem and the ability to submit it to God is humility. People who are humble have learnt to ascribe anything they achieve in life to the Author and Finisher of our faith. They ascribe all their successes to the glory of God. They do nothing out of selfish ambition or vain conceit but in humility consider others better than themselves (Philippians 2:3-4).

God despises pride and multiplies His grace on the humble (1 Peter 5:5). There are many people with grandiose delusions, flamboyance and pompous attitudes. They find it difficult to ascribe their achievements to God. Such people are called fools in Luke 12:16-20.

I have found out that God fights and defends His humble children. When Moses married a foreign woman, Miriam and Aaron complained about it but God defended His servant because Moses was faithful and humble. It is one thing to be faithful but it is another thing to be humble. Many have lost the grace of God as a result of pride. In the middle of Miriam and Aaron's discussion, God showed up suddenly to defend His humble servant. As a result of his humility, he was able to enjoy deeper communion with God. He saw God face to face.

Numbers 12:6-8 NLT
"The LORD said to them, "Now listen to what I say:
"If there were prophets among you, I, the LORD,
would reveal myself in visions. I would speak to
them in dreams. But not with my servant Moses. Of
all my house, he is the one I trust. I speak to him
face to face, clearly, and not in riddles! He sees the
LORD as he is."

What a level of grace!

Holiness is a process of being pure like God. It is
perfected on a daily basis. Grace flows in a pure vessel.
The Bible says God is too pure to behold iniquities
(Habakkuk 1:13-14). Paul emphatically says grace cannot
increase if we continue in sin (Romans 6:1-2). God is holy
and has challenged all His children to be like Him. God
cannot use a filthy person and God issued this warning
in Leviticus 21:16-17.

The greatest weapon the devil uses against the
church and God's people is compromise. Some Christians
allow their environment to change them and it affects
the way they talk, dress, behave and even raise their
children. Society enforces her tradition on the church
and the church begins to speak fear instead of faith. A
vessel that wants to increase in grace cannot play games
with God because He knows everything. God cannot be
deceived and will not compromise His standards with
anyone. We should run from every appearance of evil
and forsake sinful activities and associations. Run from
sin if you want God to multiply His grace in your life.
When you are holy, God will guard you as the apple of

His eyes. 2 Timothy 2:19 says:

> "Nevertheless the solid foundation of God stands, having this seal: "The Lord knows those who are His," and, "Let everyone who names the name of Christ depart from iniquity."

The devil always looks for people who have his traits or possessions. Jesus boldly declared His holy living by saying in John 14:30 NIV "I will not speak with you much longer, for the prince of this world is coming. He has no hold on me." The devil could not find lies, cheating, falsehood, pride, hate, unforgiveness or fear in Jesus. Hence, he could not hinder the multiplication of God's grace in His life.

A heart of thankfulness opens the door to God's presence and warehouse. Jesus Christ created a habit of thankfulness. When he raised Lazarus from the dead, He prayed: "Father, I thank you that you have heard me" (John 11:41 NIV). When 4000 people were hungry, He "took the seven loaves and the fish, and when he had given thanks, he broke them and gave them to the disciples, and they in turn to the people" (Matthew 15:36 NIV). Again, when 5000 people were hungry, He "took the loaves, gave thanks, and distributed to those who were seated as much as they wanted. He did the same with the fish" (John 6:11 NIV).

A deep thinker will appreciate God. Psalm 100:4 (NIV) says, "Enter his gates with thanksgiving and his courts with praise; give thanks to him and praise his name." When you are in critical need, don't panic but thank God. How do you respond to difficult situations?

Thanksgiving portrays faith. Faith moves God's hand and when you give God thanks in difficult situations, it means you believe God is above the situation. Paul lived a life of thanksgiving. He said in 1 Thessalonians 5:18 that, "in everything give thanks; for this is the will of God in Christ Jesus for you."

What is everything? Everything is everything. If you have a desire to know God's will in your life, give thanks. If you want the grace of God to increase in your life, give thanks. Thanksgiving is a door opener. We open the door to God's will by giving thanks. Thankfulness is an antidote to anxiety. Philippians 4:6 says, "Be anxious for nothing, but in everything by prayer and supplication, with thanksgiving, let your requests be made known to God."

You therefore, my son, be strong
in the grace that is in Christ Jesus.

2 Timothy 2:1

⌇ Epilogue ⌇
Be Defined
by GRACE

Many people are defined by their career, while others are known by their wealth, action or character. Judas Iscariot is known as a betrayer; Demas is known as being worldly or known for his love of the world; Jonah as a sleeper; Thomas as a doubter; but Paul is defined by grace. Paul says in 1 Corinthians 15:10 NIV that "But by the grace of God I am what I am, and his grace to me was not without effect."

When you are defined by grace, you will no longer be absorbed by the things of this world and every achievement will be attributed to God. Noah was defined by grace and lived to please God and "Noah found grace in the eyes of the LORD" (Genesis 6:8). He did everything the LORD told him to do. When God asked Noah to build an ark because He wanted to wipe off all the evil people of the earth (Genesis 6:13-21), I can imagine the ridicule, criticism, insults, abuses, and threats he must have received from people. He purposed to obey God rather than men. He was not influenced by man's opinions and was ready to be the lonely voice. Noah obeyed God to the last detail.

The grace of God produces people after God's kind. When Moses saw God, people began to see the glory of God on Moses' face. The experience with God brought a new level of exposure that could be seen on his face (Exodus 34: 29-35).

Be Taught by Grace

To be taught by grace is to be fully submissive to Jesus Christ and be led by the Holy Spirit. Romans 13:14 says: "But put on the Lord Jesus Christ, and make no provision for the flesh, to *fulfill* its lusts." Paul showed us the secret of pleasing God and that is to be taught by the grace of God. Jesus came to the world as the grace of God in order to defeat the plans and purposes of the devil. The devil is behind all the evils and atrocities of the world. 1 John 3:8 says, "He who sins is of the devil, for the devil has sinned from the beginning. For this purpose the Son of God was manifested, that He might destroy the works of the devil."

Don't Squander Grace

To squander the grace of God is to fold our hands and bury our gifts or talents given to us. 2 Corinthians 6:1 NLT says, "As God's partners, we beg you not to accept this marvelous gift of God's kindness and then ignore it." Grace and gifts go together. Ephesians 4:7 says,

"But to each one of us grace was given according to the measure of Christ's gift." The reason is to be able to serve. Many people have grace and refuse to serve. God wants us to profit in the kingdom.

In John 4, Jesus spoke to a woman by the well in Samaria who had divorced five times and lived in a common law relationship with the sixth man. Even Jesus' disciples judged her and wondered why their Master spoke with her. However, she was saved by God's grace and became an evangelist. "Many of the Samaritans from that town believed in Him because of the woman's testimony, "He told me everything I ever did" (John 4:39 NIV).

Judas Iscariot tasted grace and squandered it. He dined with the Master Jesus and even was entrusted with the Master's money (he was-chosen as the treasurer). For thirty shekels of silver, he betrayed his master and later committed suicide (Matthew 27:1-5). Judas had the privilege of knowing Him; experienced His power and saw His miracles first hand but misused the grace conferred on him. Judas' life shows us that it is possible to be so rich in grace and still live a wasteful life.

Desire Grace

Desire the spirit of supplication and grace as promised by our Lord in Zechariah 12:10 which says: "And I will pour on the house of David and on the inhabitants of Jerusalem the Spirit of grace and supplication; then they will look on me whom they pierced. "The throne of grace is always open and you will never be greeted with a busy signal or a voice message. It is God's warehouse and contains anything we need to live and walk the journey of destiny.

Grace will settle everything in life. God will always fulfill what He promises. Grace cannot be overdrawn in His account and the more we ask, the more we receive. He is more than capable and ready to give us grace abundantly. We should not relent in asking for more and more grace. The onus is on us to approach this throne for help in our time of need.

Sow Seeds of Kindness

As God gives us grace freely, we too can start sowing kindness into people's lives. The world will be a better place if tongue lashing, curses condemnation and victimization can be replaced with kindness. Sow seeds of favor and you will be greatly surprised by the harvest. King David woke up one day and decided to show kindness on the household of Saul for Jonathan's sake (2 Samuel 9:1). Saul was an enemy of David and tried many times to kill David prematurely. God's grace kept David alive. Saul did not keep his hatred for David secret and was even ready to kill his son, Jonathan because Jonathan was David's friend and tried to convince his father to change his mind. Jonathan sowed seeds of love and loyalty to David and the harvest was mighty. Even when Jonathan was long dead, his generation was preserved!

In my years of ministry, four youths have left indelible marks on my life. They all come from the same womb, quiet, reliable, intelligent, faithful and well-behaved. They are youths every pastor would love to shepherd and work with. My wife and I always appreciate the grace of God in their lives. I later found out that their parents are not just Christians but stood solidly behind their pastor when he faced challenges. They were loyal and supported him wholeheartedly. These seeds sown into their pastor's life have produced the fruits of uncommon favor on these children.

Finally, I beseech you to *grow in grace*. God releases grace in phases. We need to grow in every phase of grace. Be faithful and obedient to God in all phases. David first tested the sling on birds, lions and bears before using it to kill Goliath. As you are faithful in one phase of grace, God will promote you to another phase. Many people are not growing in grace because of impatience. If you are not patient with the phase of grace you are enjoying, you will operate in the flesh. Don't hasten to do things God has not instructed you to do but rather be in line with God. It is possible to make mistakes as you grow in grace but God will not kill you. Instead, let God work out your mistakes for His good. Don't condemn yourself but go to God and confess your faults. He will lift you up even in your mess and empower you with more grace to carry on your assignment.

Are you down? Please don't be. Look to God. Micah 7:7-8 says, "But as for me, I will look to the Lord and confident in Him I will keep watch; I will wait with hope and expectancy for the God of my salvation; my God will hear me. Rejoice not against me, O my enemy! When I fall, I shall arise; when I sit in darkness, the Lord shall be a light to me."

When Peter encouraged the church to grow in grace

(2 Peter 3:18), he spoke out of firsthand experience. When he denied the minister, it was grace that brought him back to the fold and his rightful position of a leader. When he abandoned the ministry and misled the disciples back to their old vocation of fishing, it was grace that located him, restored him and re-commissioned him (John 21). Paul also prayed for grace and peace upon the church in almost all his epistles. The reason is that Paul knew the impact of grace in his life and ministry.

Therefore, I pray the grace of God be multiplied in your life, home, family, career, business, ministry, endeavors, land and all that is yours in Jesus name, Amen.

Afterword

The dictionary defines grace as the unmerited favor of God toward men. This does not do justice to the richness of the biblical use of the term, which appears scores of times. Grace is the favor God shows to men because Christ died for them: "by grace are ye saved" Ephesians 2:8. Because of His holy character, God could not save men simply because of His mercy and love. The claims of divine righteousness had to be satisfied before He could save sinful men, therefore Christ died in the place of the ungodly (Romans 5:6).

The late Moody Bible Institute Greek scholar Kenneth Wuest defined "grace" as a "favor freely done, without claim or expectation of return." Wuest further declared that in pagan Greece, this favor was always done for a friend, never an enemy. However, in the New Testament, it takes an infinite leap forward; a meaning it never had in pagan Greece. God's saving grace expressed at the cross is targeted at those who are His enemies (Romans 5:10).

The contrast between God's nature and ours is highlighted throughout the Bible through His attribute of mercy. When Paul describes God as "rich in mercy" in Ephesians 2:4, he is indicating that God extends Himself to us especially to overcome our human frailty. When we cannot help ourselves, His mercy brings His goodness to us. However, our greater need is to have God reach out to us to overcome our sinfulness. This act is described as His grace. In fact, it comes toward the elect so abundantly that it seems like an overflowing treasure (Ephesians 1:7-8). It is amazing that God would show grace and mercy and love toward sinners but He extends Himself through these characteristics continually, often over long periods of time as in the case of many in Scriptures and Church history.

It is this which is referred to in this book as *The Highest Common Factor*. John Newton, when asked his opinion on some subject, replied, "When I was young I was sure of many things; there are only two things of which I am sure now: one is, that I am a miserable sinner; and the other, that Jesus Christ is an all-sufficient Savior. The grace of God which is given to us as described in this book brings into our lives all the ingredients for a fulfilling life. With it you do not need anything else; without it, you have nothing. It covers every area of need and requirement for life as it can be on the highest level.

Sometime before John Newton's death, his sight became very dim and he could no longer read. A friend and brother in the ministry called to have breakfast with him. Their custom was to read the Word of God following mealtime, after which Newton would make a few short remarks on the Biblical passage, and then appropriate prayer would be offered. However, on that particular day there was silence after the words of Scripture "by the grace of God I am what I am" were read (1 Corinthians 15:10). Finally, after several minutes, Newton spoke, "I am not what I ought to be! How imperfect and deficient I am! I am not what I wish to be, although I abhor that which is evil and would cleave to what is good! I am not what I hope to be, but soon I shall be out of mortality and with it all sin and imperfection. Though I am not what I ought to be, nor what I wish to be, nor yet what I hope to be, I can truly say I am not what I once was: a slave to sin and Satan. I can heartily join with the apostle and acknowledge that by the grace of God I am what I am!" Then, after a pause, he said. "Now let us pray!"

Using a number of examples, Dr. Dada has shown the significance, value and place of grace at various stages with reference to many biblical characters and contemporary people. This brings the subject home to anyone regardless of preferences. It is a remarkable, practical summary of the teaching on grace from many angles. No more should anyone make the parochial mistake of thinking grace covers only remission of sins because grace has always been and will remain an important aspect of Gods dealing with man. This book is a simple read, profound in depth, practical in relevance and a treasure to have.

Rev. George Adegboye
President, *Ever Increasing Word Ministries*
(Rhema Chapel International Churches)

Grace Notes

❦ God decorates a humble heart with His ornament of grace.

❦ Grace strengthens us to survive the struggles of life.

❦ Grace stills the storms of life

❦ A dose of grace will boost your vitality.

❦ With grace you will never burn in the furnace of affliction

❦ God may not give gold but He will always give grace.

❦ Grace will make your words a wonder to the world.

❦ Grace disgraces evil.

❦ Grace covers our mistakes and causes us to begin afresh.

❦ Grace opens God's heavenly doors for continuous flow of His blessings.

Acknowledgments

I am grateful to God for the grace bestowed on me to birth this message and the successful completion of the book.

I appreciate my spiritual parents, Daddy and Mommy Adeboye for their blessings and prayers.

I am grateful for the kindness, counsel and prayer of Pastor James Fadele and Pastor Tosin Macauley.

I must thank Dr. Sam Chand and Rev. George Adegboye for their spiritual guidance; and for writing the foreword and afterword respectively.

Some of my friends have given me moral support, advice and shown tremendous love in my hour of need. Thanks to Foluso and Biodun Ola for being true friends indeed. I also thank Pastor Bode and Kemi Akindele for their assistance in reading through the manuscript and their encouragement in making sure this gift is not buried.

I must thank Dr. Ben and Belinda Enoma for their guidance, patience and insights in getting the work published. My editor's attention to details and expertise has made the work thorough and interesting to finish.

I salute all my spiritual children worldwide who are aligning with the grace of God in my life. May the Father's blessings and grace be multiplied in your lives.

Lastly but not the least, I sincerely appreciate my four children: Timothy, Esther, Mary-Favor and Deborah-Peace for their love, patience and understanding when engrossed with the work. You are the best and I cherish our moments together.

Notes

Notes

Notes

Notes

Notes

Notes

We want to hear from you.

Have you experienced abundant grace that surpasses all understanding? Tell us about it. Please send your stories to *info@dunamispress.com*

Other resources by Dr. Olayinka Dada

UNLOCKING DIVINE DOORS:
How to receive a life-transforming visit from God
www.unlockingdivinedoors.com

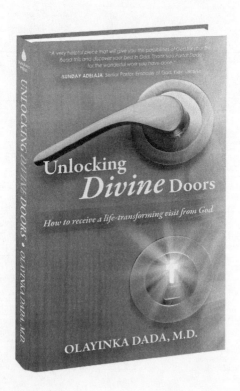